# Jenny Mitchell

# Her Lost Language

Indigo Dreams Publishing

First Edition: Her Lost Language
First published in Great Britain in 2019 by:
Indigo Dreams Publishing
24, Forest Houses
Cookworthy Moor
Halwill
Beaworthy
Devon
EX21 5UU

www.indigodreams.co.uk

Jenny Mitchell has asserted her right under the Copyright, Designs and Patents Act 1988 to be identified as the author of this work.
© Jenny Mitchell 2019

ISBN 978-1-912876-19-8

British Library Cataloguing in Publication Data. A CIP record for this book can be obtained from the British Library.

*This book is sold subject to the condition that it shall not, by way of trade or otherwise, be lent, re-sold, hired out, or otherwise circulated without the author's and publisher's prior consent in any form of binding or cover other than that in which it is published and without a similar condition including this condition being imposed on the subsequent purchaser.*

Designed and typeset in Palatino Linotype by Indigo Dreams.
Cover design by Ronnie Goodyer from original image part of a mural by unknown street artist, Cape Verde.
Printed and bound in Great Britain by 4edge Ltd.

Papers used by Indigo Dreams are recyclable products made from wood grown in sustainable forests following the guidance of the Forest Stewardship Council.

For Nancy Christina Downie
and Mark Anthony Mitchell

*Her Lost Language* is Jenny Mitchell's debut collection

## CONTENTS

### My Family Shares its Voices

| | |
|---|---|
| Lessons About Flight | 9 |
| Lost Child | 10 |
| Jamaican Freight | 11 |
| My Five Times Great-grandmother was Enslaved | 12 |
| A Cello Hummed | 13 |
| Song for a Former Slave | 14 |
| Blood, the Seamstress | 15 |
| Emancipating Ancestors | 16 |
| Missing Grandmother | 18 |
| Becoming Queen | 19 |
| My Family Shares its Voices | 20 |
| Deep Mourning | 21 |
| Before the Silence | 22 |
| Caribbean Service | 23 |
| Strange Land | 25 |
| The Bride | 26 |
| A Veil | 27 |
| The Mess They Made | 28 |
| Monica Darling | 29 |
| Ugly Close to Sleep | 30 |
| This is Not My Mother | 31 |
| Retreat, Jamaica (1939) | 32 |
| Taking His Leave | 33 |
| Someone Thank the Tailor | 34 |
| Out to Sea | 35 |
| When He Died | 36 |

**Eve's Lost Daughter**

The Imaginary Table ............................................................... 38
Hansel, Gretel and the Witch ................................................ 39
Cut from Genesis..................................................................... 40
Eve's Lost Daughter................................................................ 42
Dark Sisterhood ...................................................................... 43
The Healing.............................................................................. 44
English Fields .......................................................................... 46
Unfurling.................................................................................. 48
Black Men Should Wear Colour............................................ 49
A Million Suns......................................................................... 50
Incident..................................................................................... 51
Her Lost Language..................................................................52

# Her Lost Language

## Lessons About Flight

Freedom in the air was what he described first,
my father: how gliding on God-given breeze made escape
so easy for the birds – a long forgotten name.
They simply flew above the shot.

Calm in their description too:
neat, red and yellow plumage.
The devil's strength in smooth, grey claws,
rarely glimpsed above the blue Jamaican hills.

Their song, so strangely loud, helped fell the sugar cane
for slaves exhausted in the fields. These men and women hid
to rest from overseers, soaking up the sound;
hummed a softer tune at night to lull the birds to sleep.

This mutual help was stopped by men, as white as waves.
Guns cocked, they gained their stature
stopping breath close to the ground. Father says the birds
looked at the mounting dead but flew serene.

His voice grew more serene. I pictured them as clouds
made from the brightest colours, high above a damaged world.
He said they were cheered on their long, lost way
by those who came before us in the fields.

## Lost Child

Washed up on a gleaming shore,
a necklace of small stones,
not pearls or sea-made precious things
but shards washed smooth
by centuries beneath the churning water.

The twine that held the stones
survived intact somehow – so short
it must have circled a child's neck –
a daughter thrown with all the rest,
overboard in chains,

black bodies sacrificed as ballast
to be ditched or self-destroyed.
They clambered out of reach
to swim back home, go to their God,
demand an explanation.

These stones, reclaimed
by human hands,
hold colours we have never known,
can't speak about the child
except to say
she was such treasure lost at sea.

## Jamaican Freight

Loss was what I thought of first,
when looking at the sea;
thinner waves than yesterday;
tide's frayed hem pulled so far up,
exposing wrinkled knees.

Immodest surf –
once an astonishment of pearls,
now barely strung
across the slack horizon's neck,
choking on a hotel dragon's fumes.

They swell across the beach –
less sand than human debris,
to show what can't degrade
does so entirely.

Heels alight on jagged claws:
tin gods demanding human blood,
sacrificed to dirt-flecked foam.

Poor water,
shying back – receding hope –
exposing all the dead – marine
and stranger freight:
remains of stolen Africans
thrown overboard in chains –
little more than language down their throats.
The last word might have been revenge.

## My Five Times Great-grandmother was Enslaved

Her legacy, held in a dress:
flimsy twist of torn green cloth,
palm-sized when wet.

Dry, it unfurled across the floor,
nudged at the threshold –
lush savannah, lion's roar;

became long rays of light
between soft folds,
released in vibrant waves.

A herd of wildebeest appeared.
Their backs dislodged my ceiling –
rubble and cascading leaves.

The forest round the hem
led to a valley of blue hills,
on towards a trembling lake.

Beyond it stood her long-lost home:
a hut with windows, pocket-sized,
the dark rip of a doorway.

Inside, the seams were packed
with voices just like mine.
They rose as one towards me.

## A Cello Hummed

When the music started,
I wanted it to go a different way.

The violins should sway
towards a gentle light,

not hurry to attack
my fragile calm,

become a soldier's march
when I so longed for peace.

Underneath, a cello hummed,
strings suffering.

## Song for a Former Slave

Her dress is made of music
humming through the hem,
high notes in the seams.

A rousing hymn
adorns the bodice
with sheer lace.

The heart is stitched with loud amens,
the back a curving shape
of hallelujahs.

She's proud enough to hold
her own applause
tucked in a pleated waist.

The skirt sways freely
when she walks
to show there are no chains.

Her dress is made of music.

## Blood, the Seamstress
*for my maternal grandmother*

I'll be the dress she never owned –
immaculate for special days,
the only burden heavy frills,
and English lace along the hem.

I'll never trail in dirt
or suffer dust from cane fields.

My heart will burst to make a bodice
stitched with bold Jamaican flowers:
yellow orchids, red hibiscus.

There will be a giant fern appliqued on the back:
my ribcage opened to its full extent.

I'll raise my chin to form the high, firm collar –
a throat so elegant, with space to hold my voice.

I'll ask her what she really wants –
plain cuffs or golden buttons.

Underneath the dress,
I'll make myself silk underwear;
a soft and pretty petticoat.
Its one equivalent will be her newly-coddled skin.

My feet will form such dainty shoes,
and she will go like Cinderella to the ball.
But if she doesn't want the prince this time
she'll dance away without a care.

The English lace will shimmer as she moves.

## Emancipating Ancestors
*for those who died on slave plantations*

I'll free them all
by digging deep enough
to haul their battered bodies
from the years
of disturbed soil.

As they emerge –
some dark, some light –
I'll gather every part:
the shattered bones
and ancient clothes;

the smell of monthly blood
I'm sure still flows
when women young enough to breed
are killed.

I'll stroke their wasted skin,
so like my own,
and cradle every one –
my arms that wide, that strong.

The love I have for them
will be a nursery rhyme
with hushing sounds,
and promises of home.

I'll pull out all the leaves
lodged in their throats,
replace them with my words
to let them speak.

Or if repulsed
by that well-meaning force,
they're free to push my hand away.
I'll understand the leaves
help ground lost voices.

Then I will sit, a child again,
to breath their wisdom
and their weakness – all the same
if I dare open like a grave,
allowing them to seep
so deep inside,
I'll be reborn.

**Missing Grandmother**

There are no images of her.
I want to say too poor, too long ago.
But there are photographs of men she fed,
gave birth to, saw into the ground.

Perhaps she was bent double at a stream,
beating hand-me-downs against the rocks;
cooking on the open fire
snug beside the headstones in the family yard.

When the shutter snapped, smoke obscured her face.
It has never been described to me.
I want to say that's immaterial.
The past is more concerned with monumental qualities.

But surely all the children that she had –
eight lived, four died without too many words –
could muster a description of her eyes, her nose.
Her mouth won't ever say my name.

She'll never stroke my hair, or me, her skin.
Perhaps it was burnt-curling by the stark
Jamaican sun – her photograph, I mean;
abandoned in a broken chest of drawers.

There might have been some trace of tenderness
captured on her long-lost, paper face.
We have the same complexion I've been told.
So that is what remains: her shade walks with me.

## Becoming Queen

I want to make a myth:
grandmother with a soaring voice,
each word so strong she only has to say it once
for it to have its meaning.
No nagging till the volume rose
into her arm, became a palm,
brought down on childish flesh.

Her body has to be transformed.
It will not be weakened by a dozen births,
back bent from holding up a three-room shack
to till Jamaican soil.
A *labourer* on twelve certificates;
four children buried in the family yard
where very little grew.

She will be bigger than the world –
her torso made of independent states:
one breast enslaved, the other healing.
Her arms so wide and legs so long
she'll step across the stream
where she spent half her life,
kneading suds in worn thin clothes.

I'll watch her stroll across the sea to Africa.
She'll meet the stamp of her dark skin:
paupers who once captured became queens.
They'll welcome her with all the love
she did not have alive,
as she recounts the tale of her true self –
a voice that's found its meaning.

## My Family Shares its Voices

Granny says all ghosts live in the mouth,
survive on words we do not need to speak.

Sounds made in argument are long-dead,
disappointed ones, gluttons for revenge.

Grandfather's rage persists in all our throats,
his one bequest: a hail of hurtful names.

They might be soothed by drink,
tongue drowned to death, as he was in the end.

Her sighs when close to sleep are young girls
gazing at the marriage bed;

plump pillows cause a groan of hope;
desire as a breath contracts the waist.

The pain in her remaining teeth: a silent echo
of the screams she made on her first night.

So many questions cling to my soft palate,
afraid she'll say how scars met with her skin.

No language could express the rage I'd feel
at damage done before my birth.

To curse would only bring grandfather back,
enraged and impotent in all the workings of his mouth.

I close my lips instead, and join the family line:
silenced women and shamed men.

## Deep Mourning

When granny died her clothes began to speak.
Each tattered dress demanded to be burnt,
the shoes begged to be buried near the grave.

*I'll lose my way without a steady guide.*

The only pair of earrings she possessed
dived from the dressing table as if it was a cliff,
their final words a whispered prayer for Eve:

*God cover up her nakedness.*

A wedding gown, white-haired and meek,
appealed to be sent back to granny's former life:
Jamaica long ago, where she was happy last.

*We'll dance like foam across the Caribbean Sea.*

Her nightdress answered wearily:

*It's such a lovely dream, but as she's deep in British dirt
there doesn't seem much hope of that.
Please tell me how to rest without her now?*

**Before the Silence**

They were not my parents when they first held hands,
pushed up against a corrugated shack,
her breathless with the shock: his body,
a hard shape pressed to her floral waist.
Jamaica hummed with mounting heat.

Grandfather-in-the-future – formal when he wasn't drunk.
A village lord – medal from the First World War
wrapped in newspaper crackling with rats.
He threatened any *pup* who sniffed around his girls.
Must have been at work when the lovers dared.

My father, though he wasn't yet,
gently kissed her cheek, breathed against her neck,
whispered love he learnt in films:
*No words can ever say how much.*
She didn't know she had a spine to chill.

Her head lay on his shoulder – bony, I would learn in time.
They fell on stony ground, a sweat of perfect, obscene shapes.
She called his name; he put a hand across her mouth,
afraid of *catching licks*. Gulls screamed
above the house near Kingston harbour.

Grandmother-who-I-never-met guessed about the child –
a straining dress; screamed a clump of hair,
showed it to her husband. He sat beside the open fire,
bottle shining in the flames.
Never said another word to mother-in-the-future.

## Caribbean Service

Ever since I first taste words,
none as succulent as *England*,
served between the heat-damp pages
of my schoolbooks,
held up like a looking-glass to hide
the corrugated shacks
pressed hard against Jamaican hills.

Graveyards growing in the garden.
Old familiar bones pushed
through the soil – *duppified* the crop.

Daddy forced to work in U.S. fields.
Mummy washed the neighbours' clothes,
bent so often in the stream
her face resembled pummelled rock.

Pennies saved so I, the only girl,
could eat more books;
brought up in exams
until the Mother Country offered
me a role – not high but loyal:
to nurse its remnants from the war.

Happiness could not describe the day I left
the old ones crying on the dock,
rail pressed so hard against my waist,
I tasted metal on my tongue.

Didn't know the heat was held
beneath my skin till it began to ebb away,
closer to the greying shore.
Bladder weak with cold.
Sun the colour of my urine.

Disembarked at night; uniform too tight –
made a scratching sound with every step
inside the ward of disapproving faces,
daring to spit *monkey* when I held them
to my breast, just to clean their shit.

Wouldn't eat the food
if I had touched the plate.

Cried alone in my bed-sitting room,
haunted by the ghost of paraffin.
Burn marks on my legs;
always edging closer.

## Strange Land

Great Britain / 1963 / winter / known as The Big Freeze / I see mummy / slipping down a gangplank / in a thin coat / balancing a lace hat / curled up invitation in one hand / chain tied to the other / trapped between Jamaica / *No more money left for school* / and a hotel in Bayswater / *Maids sleep in the roof* / forced to wear a uniform / scrubbing floors to pay her rent / no rest for a *Christianable* woman / mind enslaved / believed hard work was close to God

Daddy / twelve years older / stretchered bloody men to end the war / another *darkie* settled here / lauding education / shared a room in Notting Hill with mice / swapped his army uniform for a factory overall / trapped outside a pub by teddy boys / *You're all a bunch of ugly monkeys* / fists like paving stones / daddy haunts the Veterans' Club for safety / slaps down dominoes till the table cracks / skin too hot with rum / sweating white dots off the black / studying at night / he fails

Church on Sunday to lament / *How can we sing the Lord's song in a strange land* / he joins the queue for the free lunch / *Bless you my son* / mummy piles food on his plate / he smiles at her like Jesus / *What a pretty dress* / walks her to his freezing room / naked bodies melt / icicles drip off her pregnant belly / *Father I have sinned* / forced to say *I do* / every year another *blasted pickney* / daddy runs away / mind enslaved / believed all free men lived alone

This winter / mummy sent to hospital again / voice grown weak with telling off / raised us with a leather belt / backbone pulled out / limp / held tight / silence as a final punishment / I am trapped beside the bed / forced to hear her in my womb / *Mine was such a waste of life / longing for the sun / he smiled at me like Jesus / what a pretty dress / nothing more to add / if God meant me to talk about the past / he would have punched a hole into my gut / let the words spill out*

# The Bride

I've seen the wedding photograph
that proves my mother used to laugh
before the war – head thrown back,
mouth open to the room, eyes squeezed shut.

She's sitting down, her hands on bony knees.
The office suit looks grey beneath the cloudy glass;
the modest veil is tilted or about to fall.

My father, standing at her side, is smiling at his feet –
amused, embarrassed, scared – it's hard to tell:
he never talks about the way he feels.

He's swamped within the uniform –
the collar wide, the sleeves too long;
looks like anybody's son – the simple one
who went to fight, even though he was too young.

I'd like to know what made them tick
but wouldn't want the photograph to speak.
I'd be too sad to hear they were in love,
or that the start was filled with hope.

It's just I've seen her smile so many times.
She even makes a gleeful sound,
without much strength or will.
Wonder what I've missed
not to hear her really laugh?

## A Veil

My mother held it tight
above a box marked *charity* –
shaped gossamer with pearls,
one hanging from lace string.

She spoke about the gown she *almost* bought,
neckline trimmed with satin bows –
*Big as a fist.*
*Too pretty for a girl like me.*

She squeezed the veil to make it white again,
poked a finger through the crown,
complained about the damage she had done,
threw it at her feet.

I picked it up like air or father's ashes.
She tore the veil out of my hand,
gave a sideways glance – scorned friend
threw it in a box, sealed the flap.

**The Mess They Made**

Mother first began to hoard soon after father died,
as if it helped her loneliness to make each room a cave.

Mirrors multiplied until the hall became a funhouse,
distorting cardboard boxes on the stairs.

Our living room was where her broken things
lay down to die on every dusty surface.

Each window was an inch of light behind a wardrobe
filled with bottles of cheap wine.

Last night, she grabbed a book out of a mountain.
I watched a new shape form from damaged spines.

With the family album on her knees, she touched
my father's cheek more tenderly than when he was alive.

She spoke about their drunken fights as if she missed
them more than him, and sighed.

As she turned another page, I forgot the mess she made,
sat with her in silence for a while.

## Monica Darling

No one but her
        could blow out seventy-six candles (and one for good luck)
with a single resolute breath.

When the smoke rose up to her face she frowned:
                      *Who are you calling mum?*

She will only respond to Monica Darling as if in a Noel Coward play,
not some residential home she planned to burn down
till the nurses began to call her Monica Darling as well.

They carefully place a doily on a sterling silver tray,
ensure her cup and saucer aren't chipped.

Monica Darling will only drink jasmine tea
when mum didn't care about things like that.
She raised four kids in a three-bedroom house;
worked two jobs when Dad worked nights.

Now she won't accept a hunk of cake
when she used to crave sugar so much.
It's thin slivers only, served on a bone china plate.

She's given up her cigarettes – smoking isn't ladylike;
thrown away the socks she used to wear at night.
                *Better to have chilblains than look like some old tramp.*

She was never a wife.
            *Who's that old man in the silver frame?*
            *Take out his picture, re-use the frame.*

There are days when the mention of children makes her laugh –
            *Oh, dear me no. I never went through any of that.*

Monica Darling is happy now.
She doesn't know who's she's left behind.
She sips her jasmine tea.

## Ugly Close to Sleep

We were silenced by her old age mouth
set loose between lines gouged in cheeks
she cheered to make her children weep
although she was demure before truth-telling
gave a breathless shape to final days
made her a lethal trap great gaping hole
of missing teeth refusing all things false
when that was how we got through Christmas
calling her three daughters fat aiming laughter
at plump hands as food fell back to plates
her son puffed up with his two houses caved
as we were told he wet the bed up to the age
of twelve might not be his father's son
a man she never liked much less loved
in thirty years of *haterimony* she barked a laugh
to say his need for drink grew more intense
towards the end when we believed
he had reformed her final diagnosis saw
her wage war on two siblings doubled over canes
accusing them of suffering their mother's madness
just before she ran away we thought she had died
young I feared my turn but spared to write
this down she said I would be damned to hell
she called it her new home if I used words like *sweet*
or said she suffered from dementia just because
she saved the worst for her own body called a rag
hair loose thread skin balding velvet
she was ugly close to sleep with seven dwarves
named Dirty Envy Fussy Give Me Greedy Needy Wanty
a new priest tried to bless her in the church
she spat *You are God's fool and prayers are used-up tissues*
no one understood why lying down
she cursed the bloody ceiling as too close

## This is Not My Mother

They were shocked – the friends, who hurried past
    her open coffin – no one had been warned.
Appalled to find there wasn't more to her, no longer twice the size

of the whole room – cut down by cancer to her flinty self.
    Mouth closed for once, her roaring laugh replaced
with humming silence – what remained of the dread

organ music she requested: *Breathe on me, breath of God.*
    Her cheeks, now hollowed out, still had their girlish glow,
but false – a symptom of a feeble heart or the embalmer's hand.

I chose the last dress she would ever wear, more like a sack,
    with half its contents emptied out.
The collar needed to be straightened. I could not bear

to reach across to her. The deadly eyes might open;
    line burst into mouth again.
She'd tell me not to fuss, keep still, stand back.

I watched her friends, the ones who cried and took their seats.
    They did not seem to notice me. Dry-eyed, I sang:
*Breathe on me, breath of God. Fill me with life anew.*

**Retreat, Jamaica (1939)**

My father talks about his birth as if he took extensive notes,
    not upside down, born in a tantrum.

The corrugated shack was scrubbed from crooked planks
    to sun-warped ceiling to receive the doctor –

only white for miles – headmaster, magistrate, map-maker;
    *Yes Sir* to his face, *English duppy* to his back.

Lounging on the bed, he hailed commands to the crouching
    woman by the door, sweating out her fifth.

Idly at the window-without-glass, her husband watched
    four daughters playing near the gravestones in the yard.

When stern legs slipped out, enough to show a frantic boy,
    the men shared an enamel cup of Old Master Rum.

Proud father ran to celebrate with Yes Sir's fee.
    He left the half-born, shoulders stuck.

As screams earthquaked the shack, four girls slid down a gully,
    tumbled over hills, pushed into a shebeen.

Their father stumbled back to see his son attempt his first
    short breaths, planks permanently stained.

## Taking His Leave

My father left a village the same size as his palm.
Undulating hills from wrist to thumb
plunge to a valley filled with dominating trees.
The upper branches are blue veins
when he holds out his arm.

Slap down in the middle is a stream,
winding to the family home,
perched on an index finger.
When it waves, the shack slips
further down the gulley.

Each fingernail is curved like my grandmother's mind.
With every break, she screams,
lies jagged on the floor for days.
The scratches on her skin are not self-made (she hides those well)
but wounds caused by grandfather.

He forces her upright to make him proud,
like all the village elders
with their brittle wives,
scars hidden under good,
church-going clothes.

Lines etched across my father's palm are all his siblings –
a dozen in as many years.
The oldest wears new clothes;
the young, in rags.
They fight for meat thrown into bowls.

The food is burnt but raw inside,
confusing as a mother's grudge,
her sour glance enough to curdle milk
straight from the breast until,
half-starved, my father waves a bony arm.

## Someone Thank the Tailor

Before my father died, a coat was made
with all the love he could not give.

The style was understanding;
his gentle voice helped form the weave.

A seam was stitched with real support.
Check lining gave encouragement.

The collar gained its height from absolute forgiveness.
Each button shone with honesty and grace.

An inside pocket bulged with tenderness;
another held kind words as well as patience.

The pockets on the sides contained his fulsome praise
for all my small achievements.

Wide shoulders had no need for pads
as they were neatly balanced.

Last of all, he willed the coat to me.
It's much too big. I wear it all the time.

## Out to Sea

He left me twice – the dead man known as father;
first: taller than the waves, his hand,
gnarled fish, slipped out of mine.

I watched him walk ahead of words
still cockled to my throat, too small
for anything but bubble-sounds to form.

I must have known a howl would meet the wind;
demands for him to turn
might drown.

He walked towards the shore, then stopped,
as if a body floated just in front;
turned back to wave both hands.

His hurried steps denied the space between us,
body bent to pick me up –
my weight a movement of his breath.

Now, washed up on a bed,
expression lost,
he's left me for the last time.

**When He Died**

the house awoke to mourning,
front door like a coffin –
open lid and body gone.

Every window was a six-foot hole,
dirt shovelled neatly to one side;
round shape of his shoulders.

Tables bowed with his last words.
Cutlery lay waiting for his hands.
Mugs yearned to know his lips again.

Walls were stamped with faded wreaths.
Hymns creaked down the stairs.
Banisters keened underneath my hands.

A mirror sent him back
until I did not know my face –
his eyes, his skin.

The house plants sprouted hair,
the front lawn stubbled with his beard.
Flowers pined for weeks in bed.

## The Imaginary Table

A dark, brown wooden top with spindly legs,
like someone on all fours
about to topple over,
shoved against the kitchen wall.

Three mismatched chairs
but no one sat on them to eat
as plates were thrown on trays;
they were held on knees.

It made the table like an altar, set apart.
I found brief moments after school
when I could sit and write, or worship
at an empty page – the pen my sacred object.

The stories seeped out of the wood:
a villain prowled; his victim skipped.
On seeing him, she ran towards
a twisted knot where she could hide.

The crack along one side looked like a stream.
A watermark became a crown;
the opening of a cave
where golden nuggets could be mined.

I spilt a cup of tea, and as it spread, I saw a cloud.
It wandered to become a lake
that swamped the village close to it.
The table turned into a boat;

and even though it sailed away, and I grew up,
these words were formed
out of a wooden top on spindly legs,
about to topple over.

## Hansel, Gretel and the Witch

She fed them words – their great-aunt in a shack,
    worn steps above a colony of rats –
spoke through a womb made by a mother
    who rent the children every time they grew,

till scarred, index fingers pressed to lips – not docile,
    but to bar the truth: relief would dance to see her dead.
They ran to this great-aunt, spinster in a forest near a stream –
    close to God in age, dress thin; blue felt hat:

mask of oxygen held to the children's mouths,
    inhaling stories from her head: Daniel, King of Beasts
bestowed the power to read visions; and one song:
    *After the ball was over, Nelly took out her false eye*

unfurled their laughter. Mother stamped the outside close,
    as great-aunt helped the children slide along her throat.
The shack became a ballroom. She waltzed around a table
    piled with junk. Dance transformed all sound –

no vermin crunching planks to infiltrate. Instead, a mass
    of stars crick-cracked the dark into a giant orchestra.
When the music stopped, great-aunt fell breathless
    on a wormwood chair her body made a throne.

Crooked fingers formed a steeple, praying stories
    through the gaps as mother kicked tall trees
to vanquished logs, stepped over rats, attacked worn steps,
    arms braced to grab her offspring.

## Cut from Genesis

Eve's grief at having borne a daughter
rude with language from the first.

She chose her name – this also lost –
voice raised against her mother's choice;

refused breast milk, not clamping lips,
but stating clearly: *I taste rue.*

Crawling, she enquired of the sky:
*Why conceive a fruit not meant to eat?*

*Our land is hard and full of pain.*
*Will you make hunger sweet?*

She took dumb clouds as proof the Lord,
if fact, was deaf.

No one could crush her claim,
though said close to the ground.

This triumph helped her stand to face her parents:
*Why shroud me in dull clothes?*

*A dress made out of blooms might fade*
*but have more style. I'll show you what I want.*

She made a dress of yellow orchids,
dancing at the neck each time she spoke.

Her words were leaves placed in the first book;
she read instead of doing chores.

Exhausted by this challenge, Eve commanded Adam:
*Grab the girl, pin back her arms.*

The child articulated rage, tongue grabbed,
a knife brought down to slash the agitator.

I saw that bloody scrap at birth;
it flops each time I phone my mother.

**Eve's Lost Daughter**

Her madness soaked through clothes, the elders said –
a need to run along the hem,
seams determined to stay single.

Buttons down the back defied her father's rules,
undid themselves. She wandered in the dark;
thread dangled from a sleeve.

Shoes stamped her need to climb the boundary wall:
heaped bones of women who had run before,
limbs chopped to form the shape of brick.

Her mother stripped her nightly, imprisoning in shame.
But naked she went out till elders
spoke of madness in vivacious hair.

They cut it to the scalp with jagged implements,
placed the bloody mess in flames,
as she went baying at the moon.

It shone with this advice, she heard it clearly:
*Steal back your clothes and scale the wall,*
*or be part of its fabric.*

## Dark Sisterhood

Pressed beneath the dirt so long,
her body turned to glass – clear, shapely
as the burial ground was murky, flat.

We only found her there because a beam of light
appeared last week – a headstone
shining through the barren soil.

We dug to find the source of that strange radiance,
hit upon her luminescent feet,
pointing gently to the sky.

We set aside our implements to use gloved hands,
soft fingertips – brush away the grime,
reveal the intact form.

The skin was smooth until the sun struck
at a certain slant, showed a trace
of man-made scars on every limb.

The organs should have caused disgust,
visible from brain to sex. But they were packed
so neatly: red-veined jewels.

I knelt to stare into her face – the features scratched,
so imprecise. The eyes appeared to move
though they were deep, dim holes.

The teeth, grey shards – a few knocked out –
began to part. She spoke, so crystal-clear
but in a long-lost tongue.

No one believed me then,
but now the elders weep to hear her voice.
They beg for absolution, pray for light.

**The Healing**

It happened yesterday in my home town,
at noon or thereabouts,
the sun at its full height.

We all stopped suddenly inside the shops,
or crossing roads,
to look each other in the eye.

It frightened me at first,
then seemed exactly right
for everyone to stand and wait.

I wish I'd been the first
to reach out to a stranger,
say *I love you as I love myself.*

He didn't call me mad,
or turn away and laugh.
He simply said the words as well.

I heard them echo through the trees,
settle in the highest branches.
My voice flew back to me:

*I'm tired and need to rest
but dare not if there's fear between us.
We must call a life-long truce.*

*You're free to dress the way you want,
worship as you please.
I know there's room for me to do the same.*

*The only arms we'll ever raise
will open just as wide as they can go,
reach out to end all mutual need.*

*I'll step aside when you walk down the street,*
*and hope you'll do the same for me*
*without a sense of loss.*

We nodded in agreement
that seemed too good to last
much longer than it took to speak.

But here, on this new day,
I passed a stranger
who stepped aside and smiled at me.

## English Fields

Grey-haired and stately, a woman sat beside me on a train,
despite the empty seats close by.
I thought she might be mad
when she said in a well-spoken voice:

'I was sitting alone in First Class and suddenly felt so afraid.
Funny how endless fields can pull up buried memories.
I'm sure I just heard the voices from the past,
the neighbours in my home town
who formed a shouting train of alarm
when father fell down on his way from the pub,
week days as much as weekends.

The voices called for one of his motherless brats
to go and pick him up. It was usually me as the older ones
were working late, at a dance or early married off.

I trudged past the whispering doorways,
and felt most ashamed when I came to the filthy
sack of man I used to call Dad.

He laughed in my face as I helped him stand up.
He lent on my much-lesser weight and breathed deeply.

He smelt of stale beer and sometimes of piss.
Then, young as I was, he touched my breasts
and brushed his hand on my private parts.

He looked in my eyes and dared me to speak
but the words were petrified in my throat.
His eyes were a watery green. I had felt his belt on my back.

I all-but carried him home, passed the neighbours
who cheered him on – a lush but good for a laugh.

They made their disapproval known when I married
a boy at sixteen to escape. I had to escape him as well.
There were two other husbands, and now I'm alone.

Funny, I should tell you all this.
You must have a trustworthy face.
This is my stop. Gosh that was quick.

You know, I don't believe in ghosts but if they do exist,
Father will kill me for telling the truth.'

She waved from the platform. I tapped on the glass;
then there were fields again.

## Unfurling

A man I've never seen before reached out to pull
my headwrap off close to the underground
I smelt his ripe green underarms and saw his legs
move like dark knives before I heard his laugh
a sound that cut the air as all the cloth unwound
along the road it quickly changed into a field
sown with the most outlandish colours that the sun
blinked twice short-sighted and surprised as though
its glasses were torn off but it could clearly see
for the first time a riot of blue birds on knotted trees
next to a sea of flowers raving pink some bent some proud

A woman rode past on a bike just as the headwrap billowed
dipped close to a bridge the water shining dark green fish
jumped to the surface as more cloth trailed along
the ground then whooshed up to the sky to point
at gently moving clouds that met a different sun this time
so pulsing hot it scorched the stranger's hand
he threw the headwrap down as I retied it with due care

## Black Men Should Wear Colour
*for my brother*

Black men should wear colour.
I mean an orange coat,
sunlight dripping down the sleeves.

A yellow shirt to clash with bright blue trousers –
taking inspiration from the most translucent sea.

Pink leather shoes. Fuchsias might be best
to contrast with brown skin.

Red socks should add some warmth,
so long as they're the only flames to ever touch your feet.

A tie could be mistaken for a noose,
unless you choose a rainbow swirling on your chest.

It will help to show the heart
has all the colours in the world.

Walk down any street with head held high.
I will wave my colours back and we'll both be safe.

## A Million Suns

They have risen up – the young cut down by knives
have been reborn. All wounds are healed
and skin made strong. The blood they shed
is gathered now: petals put back on their stalks;
flowers made to grow till they become a million suns.
Dazzling, they change all grief to gladness.
Stout fire burns base metal into gold –
that alchemy achieved with endless hope.

At night, the risen do not fall.
They become the moon and every star.
Fog may obscure them for a while, but have faith.
Darkness fades. Dawn comes again. The graves stand vacant.
There is no need for *Precious Child* on any headstone
when hymns are soaring voices.
Yes, the young make such a lovely chorus.

## Incident

I've come to see what remains of my son
before they wash the pavement.

There are flowers sticking out of a fence
where strangers have paid tribute –

dying leaves: a golden mass of light,
still in their plastic.

As I approach the concrete melted into blood,
a yellow-blue board screams:

*Fatal           Gang           In Confidence*

I step away from the cracks and see the guts
have said too much, each drop a part of him I knew:

the sheet where he was born,

a nose bleed on a white, white shirt;

outline of a boy with three knife wounds.

Why is it my child locked in an airless box
and not that man, frowning in his car?

Or her, a girl I do not know
and did not push into this world?

My blood has fallen on the ground.
I am the blood torn from his heart.

These strangers want to help me stand
but where he fell, this pavement,
frames me gentle enough.

## Her Lost Language

English mouths are made of cloth,
stitched, pulled apart with every word.

Her life is mispronounced.
She cooks beef jollof rice for one;

braves the dark communal hall:
a giant's throat when he is lying down.

He's swallowed muffled voices,
stale breath of food and cigarettes.

The lift is shaped by urine.
The sky's a coffin lid.

Back in her village, days from Lagos,
hills took on the shape of God,

scant clouds the colour of her tongue.
Now she must walk past ghosts who leer like men,

to eat fast food from styrofoam,
binging to forget her scars

are less important every day,
when words must match

from one assessment to the next.
Back in her block, the lift vibrates

like an assault or panic rammed
beneath her skin by soldiers taking turns.

She skypes to smile at parents
aging in their Sunday clothes.

They say more teachers have been raped.
A baobab tree is balanced on her father's head.

When the connection fails,
she flicks to channel *Save Yourself*.

A pastor bangs the podium, demands her *Hallelujah*.
She kneels to pray her papers will be stamped –

passport wrapped in green batik.
Pastor screams *Give thanks*.

## Acknowledgements

Poems in this collection have previously been published by or in association with BlazeVOX, Burgh House, Dodo Modern Poets, Interno Poesie, NWLive, Poems for Home Competition, Sarasvati, The Dawntreader, The Rialto, Trespass, Waltham Forest Poetry Competition, Ware Competition Anthology 2019.

Thanks to: Angie Barrs, Dawn Bauling, Roger Craik, David Cram, Ronnie Goodyer, Eve Gordon, Katharine Hoare, Gaynor Macdonald, Gill Scott, Giorgia Sensi, Ann Taylor.

Indigo Dreams Publishing Ltd
24, Forest Houses
Cookworthy Moor
Halwill
Beaworthy
Devon
EX21 5UU
www.indigodreams.co.uk